Science Alive

Light and Dark

Terry Jennings

A⁺
Smart Apple Media

Smart Apple Media is published by Black Rabbit Books
P.O. Box 3263, Mankato, Minnesota 56002

Printed in China

Created by Q2A Media
Series Editor: Honor Head
Book Editor: Katie Dicker
Senior Art Designers: Ashita Murgai, Nishant Mudgal
Designers: Diksha Khatri, Harleen Mehta
Picture Researcher: Poloumi Ghosh
Line Artists: Indernil Ganguly, Rishi Bhardhwaj
Illustrators: Kusum Kala, Manish Prasad, Sanyogita Lal

Library of Congress Cataloging-in-Publication Data

Jennings, Terry J.
Light and dark / Terry Jennings.
    p. cm.—(Smart apple media. Science alive)
    Summary: "Explains essential facts about light and dark, including natural and artificial light, color, and reflection. Includes experiments"—Provided by publisher.
    Includes index.
    ISBN 978-1-59920-270-9
    1. Light—Juvenile literature. 2. Optics—Juvenile literature. 3. Optical instruments—Juvenile literature. 4. Shades and shadows—Juvenile literature. 5. Color—Juvenile literature. I. Title.
QC360 J4634 2009
535—dc22
                                                                                    2007043680

All words in **bold** can be found in "Words to Remember" on pages 30–31.

Web site information is correct at time of going to press. However, the publishers cannot accept liability for any information or links found on third-party web sites.

Picture credits
t=top b=bottom c=center l=left r=right m=middle
Cover Images: Main Image: David Young-Wolff / Alamy   Small Image: WizData, inc. / Shutterstock:
Index Stock Imagery/ Photolibrary: 4r, mk/ Shutterstock: 6m, Yanik Chauvin/ Shutterstock: 10, Chuck Savage/ Corbis: 11m, pending:13t, JLP/ Jose Luis Pelaez/zefa/ Corbis: 13b, Ariel Skelley/ Corbis: 16l, Romilly Lockyer/ Gettyimages: 17, Trevor Bauer/ Istockphoto: 20b, Roger Ressmeyer/ Corbis: 21r, Moritz von Hacht/ Istockphoto: 25t, David Godwin: 25b, Index Stock Imagery/ Photolibrary: 26b, Chee-Onn Leong/ Shutterstock: 27b, Otmar Smit/ Shutterstock: 28b.

9 8 7 6 5 4 3 2 1

Contents

Sunlight

Our world is full of light. During the day, most of our light comes from the sun. At the end of the day it gets dark because the sun goes down.

▶ At night, it is dark because there isn't any sunlight. A flashlight can help you see at night.

Making Shadows

During the day, if you stand with your back to the sun, you may see a dark shape on the ground in front of you. This is called a **shadow.** Shadows form because light travels in straight lines. Light cannot go around things.

▲ *When the sun shines, a dark shadow of this boy appears on the ground. The sunlight cannot travel through the boy's body. The kite is made from paper. Some sunlight passes through the kite, so this shadow is not as dark.*

How Light Travels

Light travels in straight lines. It cannot bend. However, there are times when light looks as if it is bending.

▲ *In this forest, you can see rays of light traveling in straight lines. The bright sunlight is shining on the mist in the air.*

Changing Speed

Light travels faster through air than through water. When light changes speed, it also changes direction. This is why objects look broken or bent when they are placed in water.

Straw

Straw appears to be broken

Glass with water

▶ *Light rays change direction when they move from water to air. Our eyes see the light rays as a straight line, so we think the straw is broken.*

Try This...

Magic Cup

Find out how moving light rays change the objects that we see.

You Will Need
• a coin • a cup • a jug of water

(1) Put the coin in the bottom of the cup.

(2) Move away from the cup, so the coin is just out of view.

3 Slowly fill the cup with water from the jug. What can you see?

What happened?

When the coin is out of view, the sides of the cup stop the light rays from traveling from the coin to your eyes. When you fill the cup with water, the coin magically comes into view. Light rays from the coin change direction at the water's surface. The light rays can now reach your eyes and you see the coin again.

Lenses

We use **lenses** to make objects look bigger, smaller, or even nearer. Lenses do this because they cause light rays to change direction.

◀ *The lens in this magnifying glass makes the girl's eye look bigger.*

Types of Lenses

Lenses are usually made from glass or plastic. Eyeglasses are made with **convex lenses** or **concave lenses.** These lenses sharpen an image by making objects look bigger or smaller than they really are.

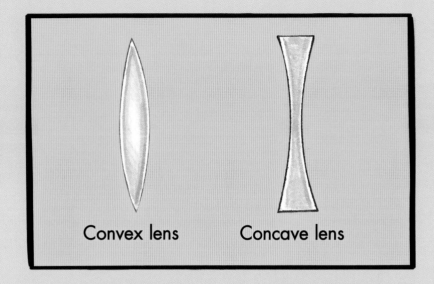

Convex lens   Concave lens

▲ *Convex lenses are wider in the middle than at the edges. Concave lenses are thinner in the middle than at the edges.*

▲ *People who are nearsighted wear glasses with concave lenses to help them see things in the distance. People who are farsighted wear glasses with convex lenses to help them see close objects.*

Lenses at Work

Lenses help us to find out more about the world around us. **Telescopes** and **microscopes** are instruments that use lenses.

Telescopes

A simple telescope is a long tube with a lens at each end. Telescopes make faraway objects seem much nearer.

▼ *Telescopes are useful for looking at objects in the distance.*

Large lens

Telescope tube

Small lens

Light rays

Microscopes

A microscope uses several lenses. It makes a small object look hundreds or thousands of times bigger than it really is.

▼ *You can see the tiny veins in a leaf with a microscope.*

▶ *With a powerful microscope like this, you can magnify objects to look at them in more detail.*

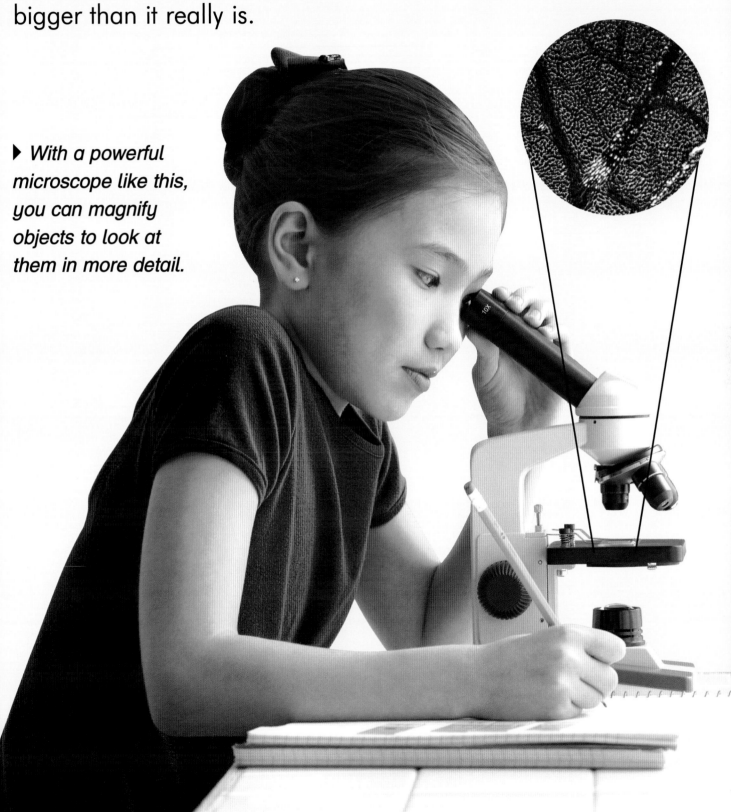

Try This...
Water Droplet Microscope

Discover how water can change the things that we see.

You Will Need
- a magazine • a sheet of plastic wrap
- water

1. Place the magazine on a firm, flat surface, such as a table. Cover the magazine with a sheet of plastic wrap.

2. Use your little finger or an eyedropper to put a drop of water on the plastic wrap.

3 What effect does the drop of water have on the illustrations in the magazine?

What happened?

The drop of water acts like a convex lens. The water magnifies the light that reflects off the paper because it causes the light rays to change direction. This makes the illustration under the water drop look bigger.

Bouncing Light

We can see our **reflection** in a **mirror**. This is because light bounces off smooth, shiny surfaces made of glass or metal.

Mirrors

Most mirrors are made of polished glass. Light rays hit this smooth surface and bounce off at the same angle, to give a reflection. When light rays hit rough surfaces, they bounce off in different directions, so they do not give a reflection.

◄ *When light hits the surface of a mirror, nearly all the light bounces back into our eyes and we see a reflection.*

Different Shaped Mirrors

Not all mirrors are flat. A **convex mirror** curves outward and makes objects looks smaller. A **concave mirror** curves inward and makes objects look bigger.

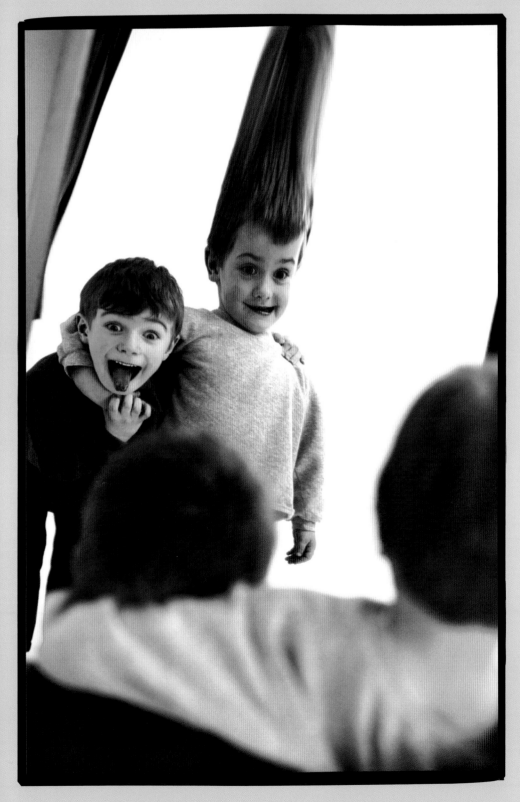

◀ *Fun house mirrors are made from convex and concave mirrors. They make people look all sorts of funny shapes and sizes.*

Try This...

Light Comb

This will show you how light reflects from a mirror.

You Will Need
- a sheet of cardboard • scissors • a comb • tape
- a sheet of dark paper • modeling clay • a flashlight
- a mirror

1 Ask an adult to cut a comb shape along one edge of the cardboard, a little smaller than the actual comb.

2 Stick the comb to the cardboard so that it covers the hole. Put the sheet of dark paper on a table and use lumps of modeling clay to stand the cardboard up at one end of the sheet of paper.

3 Shine a flashlight through the comb onto the dark paper. Hold a mirror in the path of the rays so that they bounce off it. What can you see?

What happened?

When the light shines through the comb, you can see light rays traveling in straight lines. The light rays are reflected and bounce off the mirror. If you turn the mirror, you can see that the reflections turn as well. The light rays are reflected at the same angle as they hit the mirror.

Colors

Everything around us has a color. This is because light is made up of lots of different colors.

Sunlight

Sunlight looks white but it is really a mixture of many different colors. These colors can be seen when a **rainbow** forms.

▼ *When sunlight shines through rain, the different colors in the light change direction and spread out to form a rainbow.*

Seeing Colors

Objects have different colors because light bounces off them in different ways. We see different colors when these light rays mix together.

▶ *Our eyes recognize red, green, and blue light. This balloon looks yellow because a mixture of red and green light is reflected from it.*

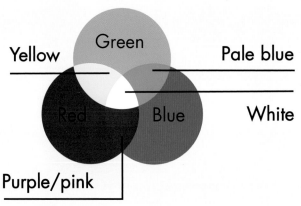

Yellow   Green   Pale blue

Red   Blue   White

Purple/pink

▲ *When red, green, and blue light mix together, we see different colors such as yellow or pale blue. When all three colors are reflected, we see white light.*

21

Try This...
Color Wheel

Look at how rainbow colors mix together to make white.

You will need
- white cardboard • scissors • a ruler • a pencil
- colored crayons or pencils (red, orange, yellow, green, blue, and purple) • tape

1 Ask an adult to cut a cardboard circle about 4 inches (10 cm) across. Use the pencil and ruler to divide the cardboard into six equal parts. Color each part to make a rainbow.

2 Push the pencil through the center of the cardboard. Put some tape on the end of the pencil. This will stop the cardboard from slipping off the pencil.

3 Hold the end of the pencil and stand it upright on a table. Spin the pencil fast. What can you see?

What happened?

When the wheel spins, all of the colors mix together and the wheel looks white. This is like the sunlight that we see. When a rainbow forms, the sunlight splits into its different colors, just like the colors of the wheel.

Light in Nature

Most of our light comes
from the sun. However,
there are other forms
of natural light. Some
animals even make
their own light.

Sun

Light rays

Earth

◀ *The sun is a huge
ball of burning gases
in space. Heat and light
rays from the sun travel
through space to reach
our Earth.*

Electric Lights

At the touch of a switch, we can turn electric light bulbs on or off. Inside a light bulb is a thin wire called a **filament.** This wire glows when the light is switched on. A light bulb is safer to use than a fire, because there is no flame that might burn us.

Glass bulb

Filament

▲ *When electricity goes through the filament, it gets so hot that it glows and gives out light.*

▲ *Electricity helps us to see at night. This city is lit up by the glow of thousands of light bulbs.*

Using Light

Light has many other uses, too. Light can be used to make electricity. The speed at which light travels also helps us to send messages around the world.

Solar Cells

Some watches and calculators are powered by sunlight. They have a **solar cell** on them that turns sunlight into electricity.

▼ *The **solar panels** on this roof use solar cells to turn sunlight into energy for the home.*

Carrying Messages

Light travels at about 186,000 miles (300,000 km) per second. This is like traveling around the world seven times in a second! When we make telephone calls or send emails, the information is stored as rays of light and travels along wires filled with very tiny **fibers** of glass or plastic.

Light rays storing information travel quickly through each fiber.

This wire contains lots of tiny fibers.

Words to Remember

Concave lenses
Lenses that are thinner in the middle than at the edges.

Convex lenses
Lenses that are wider in the middle than at the edges.

Filament
A thin wire inside a light bulb that glows when electricity runs through it.

Concave mirror
A mirror that curves inwards.

Convex mirror
A mirror that curves outwards.

Lenses
Pieces of glass or plastic with two curved surfaces.

Electricity
A type of energy we can use to make things work.

Lightning
A flash of light caused when an electrical spark jumps between clouds or between a cloud and the ground.

Fibers
Very thin strands of material.

Lightning

During a storm, flashes of **lightning** can be seen. These are sparks of **electricity.** They are even brighter than the sun, but they only last for a fraction of a second.

◀ *Flashes of lightning brighten the sky during a storm. The sparks of electricity jump from cloud to cloud or from the clouds to the ground.*

Living Lights

Some animals make their own light using chemicals inside their bodies. This is because they come out at night, or live in the dark parts of the ocean.

▶ *Glowworms give out flashes of light in the dark to attract other glowworms.*

Making Light

We can make light in lots of different ways. However, most of the light that we make comes from electricity or fire.

Fire

When something burns, it gives out light as well as heat. Before electric lights were invented, people used fires, flaming torches, or oil lamps to help them to see at night.

◀ *Fire helps to light up the dark and can be seen for miles around. Fire can also be used to cook food and to keep people warm. But fire is dangerous, and we must use it with care!*

Microscopes
Devices that make small objects look bigger.

Mirror
A sheet of glass or metal that reflects an image.

Rainbow
The colors that form when sunlight passes through rain.

Reflection
The image seen in a mirror or other smooth, shiny surfaces.

Shadow
An area of darkness caused by an object blocking the light.

Solar cell
A device used to change light into electricity.

Solar panel
A group of solar cells.

Telescopes
Devices that make distant objects look nearer.

Index

Web Finder

For Kids:

http://www.learninghaven.com/science/articles/what_is_light.htm

http://www.opticalres.com/kidoptx_f.html

http://www.sciencenewsforkids.org

For Teachers:

http://acept.la.asu.edu/PiN/act/sky/sky.shtml

http://www.can-do.com/uci/lessons99/light.html

http://www.learner.org/teacherslab/science/light/